THE

DIFFERENCE

BETWEEN

POPERY AND PROTESTANTISM.

IN A LETTER TO AN INQUIRING FRIEND.

BY "KIRWAN."

PHILADELPHIA:
PRESBYTERIAN BOARD OF PUBLICATION,
No. 265 CHESTNUT SRTEET.

Stereotyped by WM. S. SLOTE, No. 19 St. James Street,
Philadelphia.

No. 88.

THE

DIFFERENCE BETWEEN

POPERY AND PROTESTANTISM.

MY DEAR SIR:—You were educated in the church of Rome, and until recently you have received all its dogmas and teachings as true. You have been providentially led to question the truth of much that you once received with unwavering faith, and to feel that the religion of your fathers and of your youth is not the religion which God has revealed for the acceptance and the salvation of men. Because you possess not the means, nor the information for making the comparison yourself, you ask of me, for the purpose of aiding you in your inquiries after the truth, a brief statement of the difference between Popery and Protestantism. Most cheerfully do I yield to your request: and most earnestly do I pray that you may be brought from darkness to light, and from the bondage of a gloomy superstition into the glorious liberty of the children of God. The points of difference are numerous and various; but for your purpose and mine, it will be only necessary to indicate a few of them.

1. *They differ as to what is the church.* The Papist makes it to consist of all who submit to Christ and the Pope; the Protestant, of all who submit to Christ. However holy in heart, or consecrated in life, all Christians who believe not in the Pope, are heretics and schismatics in the view of Popery, and are to be regarded as infidels, Turks, and Jews! To belong to the church of Jesus Christ, it is as necessary to believe in the Pope as to believe on Jesus Christ? Can any mind, save one dyed in the mingled compound of darkness and bigotry, believe this?

2. *They differ as to the rule of faith and practice.* The Protestant asserts that the word of God is the only and the infallible rule of faith and practice. The Papist teaches that "it is not merely the written word of God, but the whole word of God both written and unwritten; in other words, Scripture and tradition, and these propounded and explained by the Catholic church."

This is a wide difference. The decisions of that small book called the Bible are final with every Protestant. This the Papist denies, and pronounces it a damning error. His rule of faith is, first the Bible, then the Apocrypha, then the traditions — the beginning and the end of which no mortal knows—then the decisions and decrees of councils, and then the interpretation of these by the church. And whether "by the church" is meant the Pope, or a council, or the Pope and council, is not yet determined. If, in some things, the Protestant rule of faith is difficult to be understood, the rule of the Papist is utterly beyond human comprehension.

3. *They differ as to the use of the Bible.* Protestants regard the Bible as the revealed will of God to man—to every man. And hence they vindicate the right of every living man to read for himself, and on his own individual responsibility to God to decide as to what it teaches, and as to what the Lord would have him to believe and to do. But Popery prohibits the general circulation of the Bible; forbids its perusal, save by those who in its opinion will not be injured by it; and supplants it among its adherents by prayer-books and missals and manuals of devotion, whose object is to supplant the religion of the Bible by the religion of the priest. Protestantism keeps burning brightly before you the light which God has kindled in our world for the guidance of our race, and teaches you to walk by it. Popery curses you for so doing, removes that light, kindles up its own, and sends you to perdition unless you walk by its dim and flickering rays.

4. *They differ as to the sole object of worship.* The Bible teaches the unity of the Godhead. In this the Papist apparently unites with the Protestant. But while the Protestant unites with the Bible in denouncing all worship offered to any being save God, or even to God by the intervention of paintings, pictures, or sculpture; Popery, on the contrary, teaches that divine worship is due to the Virgin Mary, to the true

cross, to the little piece of baked dough called the host, and that religious adoration is to be paid to angels, to departed saints, and even to relics—old bones collected from the catacombs, and, for the sake of raising their price in the bone-market, said to be the bones of saints and martyrs.

5. *They differ as to the nature of sin.* Want of conformity unto, or transgression of the divine law, is the only sin known to the Bible or forbidden in its pages. Sin is a transgression of the divine law. So Protestants believe and teach. But Popery teaches, that to transgress *its* commands is sin, and sin of the most aggravated character. It places its commands in importance above the laws of God. It is far more sinful to break Good Friday, than the Sabbath day; to eat meat on Friday, than to get drunk on Sunday; to enter a Protestant place of worship, than to go to the theatre; to read king James's Bible, than to pore over Sue's novels; to deny the infallibility of the Pope, than to burn heretics; for a priest to get married like Peter, than to keep a mistress like Herod. The violation of many of the laws of God it makes a venial offence, while it pours the vials of its anathemas upon the contemners of its precepts, and sends them to burn for ages in purgatorial fires, or for ever in the fires of hell. It makes that to be a light sin which God makes a most grievous one, and makes that to be a sin which is a positive virtue. Thus it makes void the law of God.

6. *They differ as to the agency by which the sinner is renewed.* The need of this renewal is thus taught: "Except a man be born again, he cannot see the kingdom of God." The agency by which this work is effected is thus taught: "The love of God is shed abroad in our hearts by the Holy Ghost." It requires the power which originally created man from the dust to new-create the human soul, to re-instamp on it the lost image of God. But Popery teaches, that faith with the other graces is infused into our hearts in baptism, and that they are all nurtured up to maturity by confirmation, penance, fasts, alms, the mass, and other things taught as doctrines, which are only the commandments of men. So that the Christian of the Protestant is made by God—the Christian of the Papist, by man. And the practical difference between them is oftentimes as great as is the theoretic difference as to the agency by which they are begotten anew.

If, on the Papal theory, the priest refuses to baptize, how can God make a Christian?

7. *They differ as to the way in which a sinner is saved.* When a sinner asks a Protestant what he must do to be saved, he tells him to believe in the Lord Jesus Christ, and he shall be saved. Jesus Christ came into our world to seek and to save the lost. He came not to call the righteous, but sinners to repentance; and he invites all the weary and heavy laden to himself for rest. As the blood of Christ cleanses from all sin, the Protestant sends the inquiring sinner directly to Christ, and tells him that if he believes in Christ he shall be saved. But the Papist tells him to go to confession to the priest, to do penance, to go to mass, to partake of the eucharist, to give alms—especially to the priest—to keep the holy days; and he enjoins a round of bodily service as onerous as it is unscriptural, and which, however long continued, leaves him utterly in the dark as to whether or not his many sins are forgiven. He has nothing but the word of the priest to direct or to comfort him. Is it not a wide difference whether in such a momentous affair, we have the direction of man and the comfort which he gives, or the direction of God and the comfort which flows from the direct acting of faith upon Christ, and the appropriating of his work by faith?

8. *They differ as to the mediation of Christ, as our Redeemer, with the Father.* There is nothing more plainly taught in the Bible, than that Christ is the only "mediator between God and man." "If any man sin, we have an advocate with the Father, Jesus Christ the righteous." And him the Father heareth always. This is the received doctrine of the Protestant world. Yet this part of the work of Christ is forgotten by Popery, and his mediation is thrown into the shade by the mediation of Mary, of Peter, and Paul; of the holy monks and hermits; of the holy martyrs, and virgins, and widows; of the holy doctors, bishops, and confessors; some of whom were men of God, and many of whom were men of Belial. And thus Popery turns us away from Christ, the only and all-sufficient Mediator, who is every where present to hear, and whose mediation is always prevalent, and sends us to creatures like ourselves, of limited powers, however holy, and who, if on earth at all, or near it, can hear but one at a time. There are many cases recorded

in the history of the nations of Europe, in which desperate men, giving up all hope of escaping the penalty of the law, sought to bribe the ministers of justice, or to enlist the pardoning power in their behalf through the queen and ladies of the court. Can this be the reason why the Pope, bishops, and priests all over the earth, are now crowding around Mary, and are deserting the mediatorial throne of her glorious and glorified Son, who is exalted to give repentance to Israel, and remission of sins?

9. *They differ as to the state into which souls go, on their departure from the body.* The soul of Lazarus, when he died, went to Abraham's bosom, only another name for heaven: the soul of the rich man went to hell. When Stephen was dying, he saw, through the opened heavens, Jesus standing at the right hand of God. Christ said to his sorrowing disciples, when he announced to them that his departure was near, that he was going to prepare a place for them, that where he was, there they might be also. The uniform opinion of the Protestant world is, that at death the righteous go to heaven, and the wicked to hell. But Popery teaches that the souls of the pious, after death, go to a place called purgatory, which is neither heaven nor hell, but some place between them, where they are purified by sufferings more or less protracted, and make satisfaction more or less complete for remaining sins; and that the power of the Church, the efficacy of alms by their relatives, and the influences of masses offered up, are greatly instrumental in shortening the period of their torments, and in delivering them from these awful fires.

This you will perceive is a very wide difference. This purgatory of Popery, the keys of whose doors are in the hands of the priests, is a fearful affair. It is based on the great error, that the blood of Christ is not sufficient to cleanse from all sin. It is an iniquitous delusion, devised by the priests in the dark ages, for the purpose of extorting money from poor ignorant Papists. Nothing but the doctrine of the infallibility of the church, which stereotypes error, and which is so shamelessly maintained in opposition to a world full of evidence to disprove it, prevents even the priests themselves from casting it out as a loathsome and nefarious delusion. This is the market in which souls are the merchandize, and priests are the brokers.

10. *They differ as to the object of saving faith.* The Bible makes Jesus Christ this object. He that believeth in the Lord Jesus Christ shall be saved. "He that believeth in the Son hath life; he that believeth not the Son, shall not see life." "This is the work of God, that ye believe on him whom he hath sent." In accordance with this is the teaching of the Protestant world. But Popery says, "You must believe all and every article, every point the Catholic Church requires you to believe." It also tells you, "by wilfully erring, or denying one article of your faith, you destroy your whole belief." That is, you may believe truly in Christ, and in all the Bible and the Church teach, save one dogma of the Church—as for instance, purgatory, or the infallibility of the Pope, or transubstantiation—yet, if you fail to believe any or either of these, "you destroy your whole belief," and you are lost! Is not this awful? you are lost for not believing a lie!

11. *They differ in their manner of worship.* When Christ and his apostles were in the world, their great object was to instruct the people—to teach them the doctrines which they should believe, and the duties they should perform. And when the Saviour sent out his disciples, it was with the command to "preach the gospel to every creature." They were endowed with the gift of tongues, so as to preach the gospel to all people in a language which they could understand. And hence Protestants, in every part of the world, adapt every part of their worship to the understanding of the people. Hymns of praise are sung, prayer is made, the Bible is read, in the language of the people. How different from all this is the worship of Popery. Its prayers are in Latin, which perhaps neither the priest nor one of the people understands—its chantings are in the same language, and so is its whole round of ceremony; the Mass, a most unmeaning mass of nonsense, fills up the greater part of the time; and if a word is uttered in your native tongue from the beginning to the end, it is—especially in purely Papal countries—a brief eulogy on some saint, or a brief exhortation to some superstitious observance. The worship of Protestants has for its chief ends the instruction, the conversion, the edification of the people; that of Papists overlooks all these, and fills up its hours of worship with a round of ceremonies as unmeaning as they are unscriptural, and which are

far more Pagan than Christian. Protestants know what they worship; Papists do not.

12. *They differ as to the power of the ministry.* Protestant ministers simply occupy the place which the Bible assigns them. They are set apart for the preaching of the word, the administration of ordinances, and the edifying of the body of Christ. They work no miracles, perform no charms or exorcisms, forgive no sins, absolve none from punishment. They preach salvation, through faith in Jesus Christ, to all men; they teach all men the revealed truth of God, and assure them, that by a heartfelt belief of that truth. and a life in accordance with it, they shall be saved. Far different from this are the powers claimed by Papal priests. They regenerate by baptism—they require you to confess to them all your sins—they determine the character of those sins as mortal or venial—they affix to each the kind and degree of penance they see fit—they absolve you or not at their pleasure—they create Christ, and offer him in sacrifice in the mass—and when you die, they fit you for death by rubbing you with olive-oil—they then send you to hell or purgatory, as they see fit; if to purgatory, they promise to get you out by masses proportioned, both as to price and number, to the ability of your friends to pay for them. The Protestant minister points you to heaven by a way which, like the ways that led to the cities of refuge in Israel, is open, straight, and unobstructed; upon the Papal way the priest erects his many gates, and will not let you pass one without a heavy toll. He carries at his girdle the keys of heaven and hell, and claims the power of sending you to the one place or the other at pleasure! Is not this a wide difference?

13. *They differ as to what constitutes true piety in the sight of God.* The Bible says much about being "born again;" being "renewed in the spirit of our minds;" being "created anew in Christ Jesus." These changes it attributes to the Spirit, as the agent that produces them. The love of God which presided in the heart of Adam, as he came from the hand of his Creator, was dethroned by his disobedience, and the love of sin and of self went up to its vacant seat. All true Protestants agree that the change indicated by the above texts, consists in restoring the love of God to its rightful place as the presiding affection of the soul. When, by the Holy Spirit, the love of God is shed abroad in the heart, then the

individual is "born again," is "renewed in the spirit of his mind," is "created anew in Christ Jesus." And this is, in the estimation of the Protestant, the main element of all true piety. This is a change at the fountain of all moral action, and influences all the conduct towards God and man.

How different from this is piety in the estimation of the Papist! It consists in obedience to the church—in submission to her laws—in attention to her ordinances—in the punctual performance of the ceremonies which she enjoins. If the Papist keeps lent piously, he may sin as he lists at the carnival—if he love the Pope, he may hate Protestants—if he fasts on Friday, he may feast on Sunday. The piety of the Protestant consists in a heart right in the sight of God, prompting to right conduct toward all men; that of the Papist consists in an external obedience to prescribed ceremonial rites. And when we remember that God looks not upon the outward appearance, but upon the heart, this is a wide difference. When the Jews, because of the strictness of their external observances, seemed to themselves, and to others, to be very pious, then it was that the Saviour pronounced them "white-washed sepulchres," and accused them of converting the house of God into a den of thieves. St. Ignatius made the life or death of a Moor who was riding before him to turn upon the point whether he should take one or the other of two roads, and bishops and cardinals have often gone out from what were apparently the most fervent devotions, to burn heretics. The piety of Popery is fanaticism; that of Protestants consists in the exercise of love to God and man. That of the Protestant is guided by the Bible; that of the Papist, by the church and the priest.

14. *They differ as to the Sacraments.* Protestants, taking the Bible for their rule of faith, believe in only two sacraments, baptism and the Lord's supper. By that of baptism, we are admitted to membership in the visible church; and in the Lord's supper, we commemorate the death of Christ, in obedience to his command, "This do, in remembrance of me." Every thing here is simple and scriptural. But Popery makes seven sacraments; baptism, confirmation, the eucharist, penance, extreme unction, holy orders, and matrimony. And the administration of these is accompanied by a round of ceremony as farcical as it is unscriptural, as unmeaning as it is absurd. As an illustration of all, take the

ceremony connected with baptism. The water must have been blessed on the vigils of Easter and Whit-Sunday; the priest blows thrice in the face of the person to drive out Satan—he then makes on his face and breast the sign of the cross—he then puts blessed salt into his mouth—he then "by solemn prayer and exorcisms" casts out the devil—he then lays on him "the extremity of his stole"—he then puts spittle into his ears—he then anoints him upon the breast and between the shoulders with holy oil—he then pours water upon his head three times in the form of a cross—he then anoints the top of his head with holy chrism, in the form of a cross—he then puts a white cloth upon his head—then a lighted candle in his hand, then he is baptized. And all concludes, if the subject is a child, with an admonition to the parents, "not to let the child lie in the same bed with them or with the nurse, for fear of its being overlaid!" And sublimely absurd and foolish as all this is, it is the highest sense compared with the ceremonies of the eucharist, in which the priest creates Christ out of a wafer, and while he drinks the wine himself, gives only the wafer to the people! It is through its seven sacraments that Popery debases and enslaves its people.

15. *They entirely differ as systems of salvation.* You are now an inquirer after the way of salvation. You feel that you are a sinner—that as such you deserve eternal death—that your feet are sliding on slippery places—and feeling that if your soul is lost, all is lost, the momentous question is on your lips, "What shall I do to be saved?" Protestantism has but one answer to the question: "Believe on the Lord Jesus Christ, and thou shalt be saved." And while giving you this answer, it puts the Bible into your hands as the only infallible guide in the way to glory. About all this there is no mystery, no priestly interference, no tax for the bread and water of life. Christ laid down his life to save sinners; and whosoever believes on him shall be saved, because his blood cleanses all who believe in his name from *all* sin. It was only when the last sands of life were running in his glass, that the dying thief believed on Jesus; and yet Jesus cheered his last moments by shedding down upon him the sunlight of heaven in the blessed promise, "This day shalt thou be with me in paradise." Such is true Protestantism, every where, as a system of salvation.

But how different from all this is the system of Popery.

It takes from you the Bible, and sends you to the priest. Instead of sending you to God with the confession of your sins, it sends you to the priest. Your rule of faith is the Church, and the priest tells you what the Church teaches. If you believe all the Bible, and believe fully in Christ as a Saviour, yet, if you reject any thing taught you by the priest as a doctrine of the Church, your faith is vain. It converts repentance into penance; and penance it converts into an awful sacrament, which puts you as effectually into the power of the priest, as is the bird caught in a net in the power of the fowler. And after burdening your conscience with ceremonial sins—after burdening your life with ceremonial observances—after enveloping you in the mists of her mysteries, and stupefying your senses with her gorgeous ritual—after draining your purse to enrich her priests—after so perverting your moral vision as to induce you to regard every person not a Papist as smitten by the anger of heaven, and as an heir of perdition, it only fits you after all, for purgatory, where you may burn for ages in purifying fires before you are fitted for heaven! Such are Protestantism and Popery. As maps of the way to eternal life, the one is as simple as truth, and as clear as the sun; the other is involved beyond comprehension, and as dark and remorseless as the grave. The one is the truth as it is in Jesus, the other is a damnable delusion. The aim and end of the one is to save your soul; of the other, to increase the power and riches of the priest.

Such, my friend, are some of the points of difference between Protestantism and Popery. Were it necessary, I might multiply these points of difference. But I have said enough to show you that Popery is a delusion, a fable, opposed in all its essential points to Christianity, and unworthy of a moment's confidence; and that true Protestantism is the religion of the Bible, which consults only the welfare of the sinner, and which sends him directly to the blood of Jesus Christ for salvation.

Let me request of you, in closing this epistle, to give up all matters of controversy; to forget every thing but that you are a great sinner, and that Jesus is an Almighty Saviour; and to go to him at once, humbly and fervently, saying, "Lord, I believe; help thou my unbelief." And you have this promise to encourage you: "*Him that cometh unto me, I will in no wise cast out.*"

Yours most truly, KIRWAN.

www.ingramcontent.com/pod-product-compliance
Lightning Source LLC
LaVergne TN
LVHW010833120826
845149LV00016B/1360

* 9 7 8 1 4 1 8 1 8 9 5 8 7 *